Secrets of Calabrisella

The Food. The Place. The People.

Katia Macri-Roberts

Secrets of Calabrisella
The Food. The Place. The People

First published in Australia by Katia Macri-Roberts 2022

Copyright © Katia Macri-Roberts 2022
All Rights Reserved

A catalogue record for this
book is available from the
National Library of Australia

ISBN: 978-0-646-86551-5 (pbk)

Typesetting and design by Publicious Book Publishing
Published in collaboration with Publicious Book Publishing
www.publicious.com.au

No part of this book may be reproduced in any form, by photocopying or by any electronic or mechanical means, including information storage or retrieval systems, without permission in writing from both the copyright owner and the publisher of this book.

Disclaimer: the author and publisher makes no statement, representation, or warranty about the accuracy or completeness of information contained in this book.

In memory of KittyBitty

My furry feline friend, my companion for 19 years. He inspired me to embark on this literary journey by showing me that each day can be productive, fruitful and rewarding, if you have the right people in your life to support your goals.

KittyBitty sadly passed the day I finished compiling this book. I feel he kept going to give me the guidance I needed until the very end.

Rest In Peace my beautiful boy.
2003-2022

Preface

A Satirical History of an Iconic Institution, incorporating THE most unconventional cookbook you'll ever read and a bonanza travel showcase of the Coast of the Gods, Calabria, Italy.

The Secrets of Calabrisella is a humorous, eclectic collection of memoirs from the heyday of a quaint out-of-the-way restaurant in Launceston, Tasmania. Traversing over four decades of operation, Calabrisella was a perpetual staple in people's memories. We are proud to present never seen before recipes from our menu, travel tips to Italy, and behind the scenes operations for our continued success over the years.

For 40 years, Lorenzo held his audience captive with a garlic pizza and a glass of red. Sit back, enjoy, and delight yourself with his stories and recipes from yesteryear.

~ Katia Macri-Roberts ~

Figure 1 Photo credit: A. Vallone

~ *Secrets of Calabrisella* ~

Calabrisella Restaurant. Over 40 years serving the locals and tourists with the same menu, nothing changed and that was our winning ticket right there. People don't like change. People like comfort food. People like routine, stability and familiarity. Calabrisella was a place where the whiff of garlic brought childhood memories flooding back. Smiles coming in and smiles going out made us happy. Here I sit, decaf coffee in hand, photos of the Tyrrhenian beaches surrounding my desk, listening to all those Spanish and Italian songs that I'm sure the regulars knew word for word but had no idea what they were singing, inspiring me to share the secrets, share the memories, share the stories that have fascinated many for years.

~ *Katia Macri-Roberts* ~

Covid has destroyed the world for the last two years. Destroyed the livelihoods of many hospitality and travel sectors around the world. In April 2020, Lorenzo decided it was time for us to retire. After 41 years at the helm, the hospitality world was at its knees, businesses were closing all over the country. No trading meant no revenue. In his seventies now Lorenzo and I decided this was the best time. We were on a high, and we always said we would go out with a bang. We were loved, and that's how we wanted to be remembered. Our Facebook page went crazy the day I posted our retirement. We had lovely messages, actual letters, flowers, gifts, photos and accolades from locals and around the world sent to us congratulating our achievements and wishing us all the best. Even though I am only 'young' I had been in the business for over 30 years myself and it was the perfect time to bow out with my dad beside me. Covid didn't close us, but it certainly helped make our decision. It was time. We didn't want to slip away, we wanted to always be remembered as the 'hidden gem' we were known for. It is now that Lorenzo and I recollect our heyday.

For many years we worked alongside each other, becoming local celebrities, well, maybe Lorenzo did. I can still hear the squeaking front door open forty, maybe fifty times a night. The welcoming "Ahhhhhhh Lorenzo!" emanating from the gleeful patrons excited to see the one and only jovial Calabrese immigrant, glass of wine in hand ready to deliver another intensifying chronicle of his youthful adventures around the globe. I, on the other hand, was always diligently sweating away in the hot kitchen, 15 frypans in tow, and not a pina colada in sight.

~ Secrets of Calabrisella ~

Lorenzo's penchant for cooking and creating has always been a passion from a young age. In turn, myself, his daughter, retrained in 1998 and took over the reign of the kitchen for a further twenty-two years. It is our pleasure to present to you some cherished insight of our family, our heritage, our secrets and share in our jubilation of the little-known history of Calabrisella.

We hope you enjoy partaking in the carefully selected recipe hints that adjoin our memoirs. And to set the scene, a quote from our humble Calabrese dialect: "Si voi campara anni e annuni, viviti vinu supra i maccarruni (If you want to live for long years, drink wine and eat macaroni)."

Let's go right back to the very beginning. Lorenzo, my dad, was born in Parghelia, Italy, in the region of Calabria. A very poor village in amongst meagre farmland at the end of World War II. The eldest of five children born into a two-room shanty, it wasn't unexpected that he would have to emigrate to find work to send money back to the family. My father and his father come up with a brilliant plan which meant he was on the next ship out and embarking on his fanciful career for the Princess Liners sailing the coastline of the United States.

~ *Katia Macri-Roberts* ~

Stories abound of shenanigans enroute from California to Acapulco, Mazatlán and Puerto Vallarta. His ships, the exquisite cruise liners, the "Sea Venture" and sister ship "Island Venture" were used in the 1977 hit show "The Love Boat" under the name of 'Pacific Princess'. As barman, I can honestly say he was the very first "Isaac"! It was because of this lavish west coast route that we had the ever so popular 'Prawns Mexicana' on our menu for many years. A decadent array of fresh chilli and garlic infused Black Tiger Prawns in a light fresh tomato and basil sauce with a traditional Mediterranean salad. A highly sought-after dish nobody can deny.

~ Secrets of Calabrisella ~

As time went by, a very young Lorenzo sent back more and more money to his mother in Italy to help raise his younger siblings. Over time, he managed to experience voyages to Alaska, highlighting the scenic Juneau, Skagway and Ketchikan. Even today, 50 years on, his favourite dessert is a Bombe Alaska, a staple on the Alaskan cruises. Another destination was the lush paradises of the Caribbean, featuring St Thomas, St Kitts and St Maarten, learning a variety of cultural Cajun cuisines along the way.

Based in New York City, stories have been generated of 'purchasing' single-use Cadillacs, to using a fake alter ego (which, was the sleight-of-hand of a 'flim flam artiste'.) 'Antonio Cacaccio'. This imaginary dude Antonio apparently lived at the exact same address Lorenzo grew up at in Italy, can you believe that? Imagine the incredible coincidence that these two unequivocal personalities lived in the same building. Phenomenal right? Lorenzo periodically sent back American cigarettes to his father who would then smoke every single one of them himself and most definitely not sell them, at all… His worldwide voyages also took him to Lisbon, Portugal, Teneriffe and Majorca. It was here the ever-entrepreneur Lorenzo found rare orchids to sell handsomely to the rich, glamorous elite passengers embarking on the following cruise from Genoa, Italy.

Honest to goodness, a charlatan in a sailor suit? Who would have guessed?! His smile, charm and mystical charisma would certainly dazzle the tourists.

The lifestyle was certainly one for young bachelors but soon Lorenzo's world was about to be tilted. It was soon that a very young, very ambitious, very suave Lorenzo picked up the future Mrs Lorenzo. Literally. She tripped and fell over his precariously placed orange juice stand. Go figure. Love at first sight of this dainty nurse on a world trip with friends enroute to new horizons. According to legend, Lorenzo enlisted upon a 40 day return cruise for Sitmar Cruises. Incidentally they met sailing the high seas of Bora-Bora, French Polynesia, which would eventually become our most popular seafood pasta dish.

"Spaghetti Bora Bora" a collection of shell-fish, namely fresh Tasmanian scallops, prawns, mussels, baby clams, Tasmanian smoked salmon and calamari sauted in a creamy white wine sauce. Delicious!

Living the life on cruise ships had its ups and downs. Many lucrative ups from wealthy Americans who tipped handsomely, but for the downs came a terribly homesick Lorenzo. Missing his younger brothers and sisters, he then made a personal quest to care for them indefinitely throughout their lives in some fashion. Helping his two brothers immigrate to Australia and to set up life in this country and provide them both with jobs.

~ *Secrets of Calabrisella* ~

His sisters, left back in Italy have been continuously praised and supported by Lorenzo in many ways in appreciation for them both caring for his ailing parents until their recent passing.

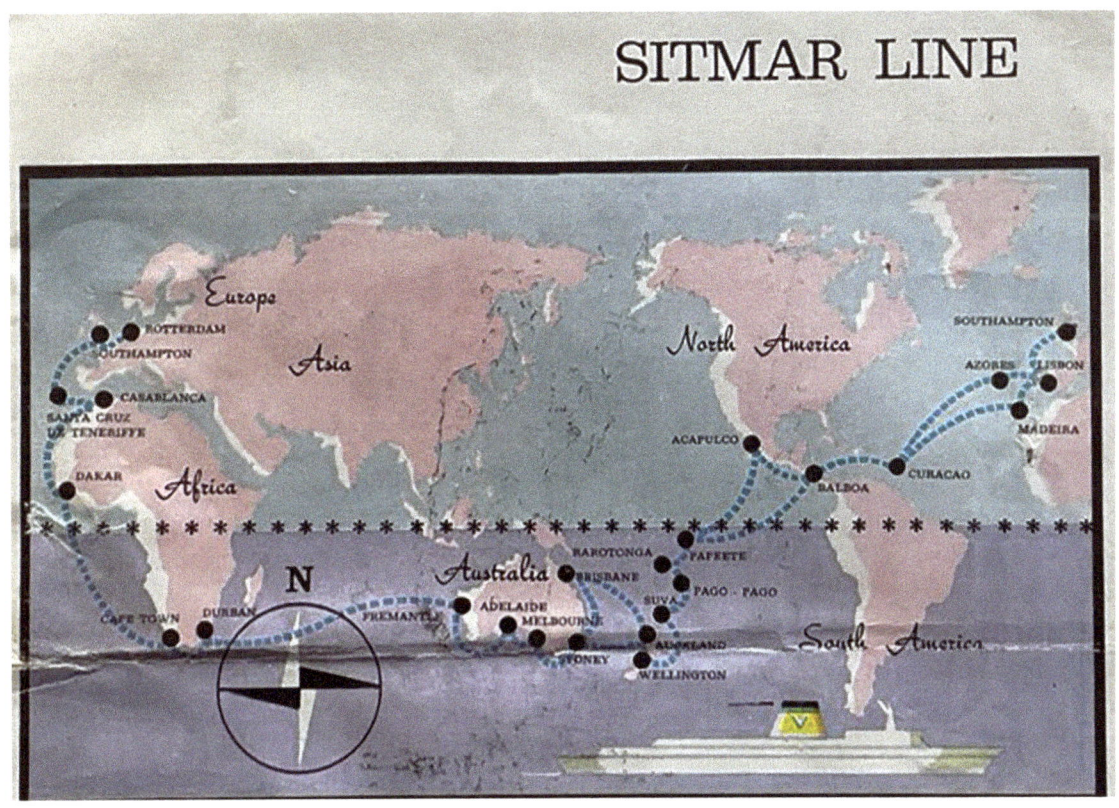

~ *Katia Macri-Roberts* ~

~ Secrets of Calabrisella ~

~ *Secrets of Calabrisella* ~

𝓣𝓱𝓮 𝓢𝓹𝓪𝓻𝓴𝓵𝓮 𝓲𝓷 𝓗𝓲𝓼 𝓔𝔂𝓮

Sigh. Where O where do I start? Oh, yes, it all started over 40 years ago. Right about now would probably be a good time to insert the front page of our menu.

"Lorenzo first established Calabrisella in the October of 1979. After previously working the Caribbean cruise ships for many years, he met his wife on board and ultimately decided to make Tasmania his new home. In the era when olive oil was something discreetly whispered for at the chemist, pesto was never heard of, and locals cringed at the concept of semi-dried tomatoes, Lorenzo took a chance. Now, after spanning 4 decades, and two room expansions, he and his daughter Katia still delight the locals with their natural talent for Mediterranean fare. Travelling back to Italy each year Lorenzo brings back local and traditional flavours from the Ionian Coast, creating inspirational signature dishes for the most dedicated aficionado of Mediterranean cuisine."

If you ever sat at one of our mismatched tables with odd cutlery, heard the smash of our pizza trays thrown passive aggressively from our ovens, tasted the intoxicating garlic or shook the hosts' hand through his "cuddle" tea-towel he goes nowhere without, then you, my friend, have lived the good life. A glass of Chianti, Italian love serenades swooning in the back round, 'Garlic Prawns' in front of you, and the ambiance of the locals. That's the best recipe for the best memories right there

~ *Katia Macri-Roberts* ~

In 1973, Lorenzo came to Australia to join the love of his life, the soon to be Mrs Lorenzo. But not before 'The" most terrifying incident occurred. In the December, Lorenzo was enroute to Fiumicino airport in Rome for his long haul flight to the far distant land of Australia. A nerve-wracking experience for any young man, leaving his motherland, his family and friends for a brand-new life. Luckily for Lorenzo his haste, disorganisation, and chaotic Roman traffic to the departure gate saved his life. Yes, his tardiness is the reason why I'm sitting here today breathing this covid ridden air of 2022. For what came next was truly devastating. It was that ill-fated day when a Palestinian terrorist group carried out a series of hi-jacks, bombings and hostage-taking attacks in Rome Fiumicino airport. Several planes were targeted and the departure hall where Lorenzo should have been waiting. He missed the massacre by minutes. Many people were killed that day, a reason why Lorenzo has a personal trepidation of airports in general. He strongly believes his local patron saint, 'San Francesco di Paola' was watching over him that day.

Sherryll, my mum, after a sojourn working as a nurse in Lausanne, Switzerland, returned to Tasmania and awaited Lorenzo's (late) arrival where he then obtained his first job in this country at Wrest Point Casino, Hobart, in the new 'revolving restaurant'. A pink bundle of joy arrived by courier stork, that would be me. Returning to Calabria in 1976, a somewhat jet-setting Katia learnt her first language, Calabrese, a helpful resource for the many trips abroad thereafter. (Except when one mistakes a diesel pump for an unleaded petrol one. There was no dialogue remotely comprehensive enough in any language guide for that bungle. And doing it in the epicentre of organised crime was a not so good idea of mine, but that's a story for another day.)

Upon our return, we migrated north to Launceston. Lorenzo obtained work at a few dining houses in town, 'Quigleys' and 'Capri'. Lorenzo then, in 1979, decided to take a chance and open his own pizza parlour. A dangerous venture for a poor immigrant back when there was no such thing as a government grant. Jeepers, no bank would touch a foreigner in those days. Funny how times have changed.

In 1979, Calabrisella was born. Over time we have grown to accept all sorts of pronunciations. 'Cabra-sellas' being the most prominent. Bit like the old "Fettuccine Cabin-ara". We embrace it, with a cheeky smile. Many people ask who or what does it mean? It translates to "a little girl from Calabria". My Dad always pertained it to connect to me and I guess I've accepted that whole-heartedly. As a 5-year-old I was made to dress up in full traditional costume and wait tables. Corny, yet effective. It made the atmosphere, the ambiance, the experience all the more authentic. (Well, so did the green and white chequered tablecloths and the stereotypical scent of garlic, but the whiny child trumps cliché ethic every time.)

~ Secrets of Calabrisella ~

As a kid, I remember peeling carrots. I remember wearing the traditional Italian folk outfit. I remember the smell of geraniums. Random, yes, but apparently, I didn't do tea parties, I played "restaurants" and had pink geraniums in wine glasses on my pretend tables. I was in it from the start I guess, or my parents had a makeshift plan to keep me occupied, one of the two.

Now, between the age of birth through to 14 I don't remember much of my dad (Lorenzo). He always worked nights and weekends and I was at school in the day. The unfortunate life of a restaurant worker, there is no family life balance. It wasn't until I started at the restaurant helping out that I really got to know my dad. Know how he ticked, knew exactly what he was trying to say. His English still isn't wonderful, but I always knew what 'the thing' was he wanted. Every micro-expression told a thousand words. Hell, even some of our long-term staff have deciphered "Lorenzo-ese" more fluently than his own family. Don't get me wrong, his umming and ahhing to this day gets him out of all sorts of predicaments.

He likes to play dumb. (As a fox.) Dad used to spend the afternoons making dough and rolling dough balls. From the pizza bench to the wall and ceiling rafter was about 5 metres. To a little kid this was like a mile away. I used to play with the dough and hurl it to see if I could make it land on the ledge. A memory stained into my brain like it was yesterday. For the next 40 years I'd walk past that ledge, look up and reminisce about those days. I hadn't started school yet. Now, I walk through the foyer and look up, reminiscing about a dough ball stuck on the ledge. I'd also remember the pile of bricks on the floor where Table 3 sits. Just through the archways. Dad had smashed the wall to make a second archway. I remember sitting on those bricks reading after school one day. It must have been about 1980. My uncle Franky had just arrived hot off the plane from Italy to start his new life here. My parents had sponsored him to immigrate and embark on a career with us at Calabrisella, to which he did for 10 years before establishing his own restaurant.

In fact, his other brother also followed in his footsteps- emigrating, working with Lorenzo for many years and then later opening his own restaurant. All three local Italian restaurants owned by the Macri brothers.

~ *Katia Macri-Roberts* ~

As time went on, I hit high school and I started to help out in the family biz. My younger brother Vincent also got dragged in to help in his teens, however he went on to follow in our mums footsteps and became an ICU nurse at the local hospital.
Hell, Dad and I dry reach just walking past a hospital, let alone work in one. We tip our hats to them, honestly. Lorenzo and I both suffer from "white coat syndrome" and let's leave it at that.

By the end of the nineties, even though I was helping out quite a bit, it was decided I'd resign from my long term day job and embark on my cooking career in 1998. I started in the kitchen and eventually Lorenzo eased his way out and took over my Front of House operations. He preferred it out front, where he could mosey about, performing his "public relations" responsibilities. For the next 22 years I would be melting away in the overwhelming heat in the kitchen in summer and he would be prancing about in the air con. Yup, lucky me. I enjoyed it though, creating new dishes, re-inventing old ones, and working behind the scenes. Lorenzo embraced the social environment exceedingly well, his favourite gesture was "salut!" and popping up in everyone's social media snaps.

Lorenzo enjoyed making friends with the customers. For those who work in hospitality know full well that there is limited if any social life or even family life. The customers became our family, we would see them more than our real family half of the time. There were many occasions when Lorenzo would find himself being invited fishing, or kayaking (that was fun), even wine-making with the customers. The impact the locals made has been truly humbling to say the least. It was not just a business venture; it was our life.

~ *Secrets of Calabrisella* ~

70's Style, 80's Décor, 90's Drama:

Who else remembers the long ostentatious gold satin curtain draped over a faux window at the back of the "Old Room"? (Once again, if you don't know what the Old Room is, I suggest you ask your parents, or maybe your grandparents) From the beginning we started with the one room, seating about 30 people. The room on the left. During the mid-eighties Lorenzo expanded, bought the building to the right and we opened up a brand new large room accommodating another 50 people. Later, in 2000, a third room opened up and some nights we could have done with a fourth!

Let's begin with a little trivia. The" Lady". Who could not know the Lady? The bizarre woman painted on the front window for 41 years. For it was this lady that everyone connected our restaurant. Who or what was Calabrisella? "It's that place with the lady on the window." We even had a staff member who, when she was a little girl, had to travel up and down the state on a bus between homes. She told us that she always passed the "lady shop" so she knew she was on the right bus. Years later she began working with us long term.

The "Lady" was a poignant Calabrese woman in traditional costume. Typically known as the "Pacchiana Calabrese", it literally translates to a person without refinement, lacking in pleasant taste, vulgar or gaudy. In some retrospect it was vulgar. Did anyone ever notice the strategically placed map of Calabria on the 'Lady's apron? Driving past there is no doubt in my mind of the phallic representation that could be easily misconstrued.

Peasant folk from the villages were more likely in history to have worn these 'provincial' garments. In actual fact, Calabria was known throughout history to provide the country with exquisite expensive silk wares to the affluent society in the 1800's. Layers upon layers of homespun silk bodices, skirts, shawls, aprons and ribbons. (Yes, the same folk outfit I as a child adorned nightly, precariously delivering pizzas to the tables). With the added spectacular prop of a tambourine, who can remember the large musical instrument prominently displayed on the wall? For it t'was that outer façade depicting a peasant villager that lived up to its name, really. Gaudy. No arguments there. But once inside the magic happened. For those that could get past the not-so-modern look, reaped the rewards of authenticity and a genuine transformation into European culture. From humble beginnings, a stellar institution evolved.

The "Room on the Left" or the "Old Room" to this day was always the most requested. For some reason, nobody liked the "room on the right" or the "big room". Was it the tall ceilings? Was it too far away from the door and you couldn't sticky beak who was coming in? Was it not squishy enough? We will never know.

Around 1999 we opened a third room, The "Girasole". Translating to 'sunflower', the Girasole was our out-door area seating a further 30 people. Excellent for private functions, with an opening roof in summer. Amazing how many people don't realise CCTV exists. Yes, the kitchen staff had fun watching the screens some nights. Shenanigans abound, especially at Christmas.

Back to our Little Room, the favourite child. Table 1 and 2 were almost impossible to obtain even weeks in advance. Right up until the end these two tables had a standing booking each Saturday night by our dear regulars. The ones who came to us for literally decades and ordered the same dishes.

~ *Secrets of Calabrisella* ~

Yes, they are the ones in the window, but I often wondered why people loved them. It's cold in winter, right near the constantly opening door. It's squishy, but you can see everyone in the room and everyone who enters, but they might not see you. I guess it's a bit like the old "back to the wall, military sniper style". I always sit back to wall, that way you can't get ambushed. But I digress…

Table One wasn't always rainbows, sparkles and unicorns either. There have been sad times, and even angry times on that somewhat quasi blissful horizon. Whether it was the average Joe Blow or a well-to-doer, people are people. What might have been a bad day for some always seemed to flip after some good old garlic pizza and Lambrusco. Troubles seem to slip away. Was it the festive Neapolitan folk songs? Could be. Was it the ambiance of the weekly theatre-goers? Maybe. Or was it just a place people could relax, be themselves, and forget their worries? Yes indeedy.

Over the years there were so many "Table oners". My Old Mate!' or 'Mi Amigo!' was a reoccurring yet rather innocuous sentiment that was often heard throughout the night when familiar faces entered the building. So much easier than remembering names. 'My Friend' was another, then bursting into salutations enroute to their favourite wobbly table rummaging for their bottle of plonk. Nothing pretentious, we welcomed everyone, even the lawyers and doctors sometimes came in their gardening clothes. Who cares, their cash works just as well no matter what they were wearing, and methinks they liked the ability to relax and be themselves.

Over time these characters noticed every crack in the wall. Every new splash of paint, every new bowl or glass. To them this place was their comfort zone. A place they grew up in, a place of happy memories. They had high expectations that we had to meet. Not for the food, no, but for the regularity and conformity. Everything had to be just so. Our menu never changed, the table array never changed, the owners never changed. Consistency is the key. Human nature is, well, to provoke a philosophical debate, a sub-culture moulded by characteristics of romantic idealisms, yet by not oversimplifying the concept of traditionalising realistic values and benevolence. What this all means is, "I'll order the Chicken Cacciatora please" (because I've ordered it every time in the last 30 years, it comes out the same, I feel good and safe, and I sleep well with a rested mind after I have it.) OCD maybe, but then we would be delving into the realms of Marx, Freud and Darwin for sure.

Maybe there are more people out there that are just as superstitious as I am? (if that is even possible) Perhaps if Mister Joe Blow changes his order from Garlic Calamari to Scallops Zaffirelli then the world as we know it will end? I'm glad they never took that risk.

~ *Katia Macri-Roberts* ~

If you can't stand the heat, get out of the pizza bar!

Friday night. Pizza night. Football night. Back in the early days, we had a dude and a rolling pin. Yes, a rolling pin. Now for the young'uns out there, a rolling pin is something one uses to flatten the dough into a round shape forming a pizza. No machines, no pre-packaged bases. The real deal. So, that meant it was a constant roll, roll, roll. Good for the biceps, no Gym membership required.

Over time we've had loads of 'personalities' in the pizza bar. From South African to Malaysian to Nepalese to Italian to French to Bhutanese to locals.

Colourful language in all tongues, but they all handled the heat, until they didn't. It's a stressful area with a lot of pressure, but a fulfilling and fun job for those who saw the light-hearted side of it. A great area to see the sights, have a chat and welcome the festivities. For the pizza bar was the place to be, especially on nights like Cup Day, New Years Eve or Valentine's Day. It's a great thing knowing Big Brother wasn't so big in the eighties!

Hurling the pizzas was another rare oddity that isn't seen these days. Throwing the pizzas aerates the dough and stretches the circumference just so. A skill that must be learnt to be a world class "pizzaiolo". They even have worldwide competitions to exhibit these particular skills. Usually held in the bustling city of Napoli (Naples) the original birthplace of the modern-day pizza. It was here that the 'Margarita' was created in honour of Queen Margarita of Savoy, the Queen Consort of Umberto I. She requested a pizza to uphold the tri-colore, the three colours of the Italian flag. Fresh basil for the "green", Buffalo mozzarella for the 'White" and San Marzano tomatoes for the "Red". I must say, we did alter our Margarita by adding anchovies and olives which confused the heck out of international tourists. I'm sure the Regina Herself would be mortified.

~ *Secrets of Calabrisella* ~

Our pizzas were unique, rustic, flavoursome and home-made. We made the dough, we rolled the bases, we chopped all the ingredients. Day in day out, for 41 years. We had it down pat, we could do it blindfolded, handcuffed and under water. But, each pizza was different each time, and that's how people knew it was fresh.

Our garlic pizza bread first made an appearance in 1979. It wasn't til the early nineties that other places cottoned on it was a winner, and to this day, people still ask for the instructions on how to get the correct balance of tart versus sweet aroma.

I often wonder about our regulars in the takeaway area, how they are, what they are up to. You may think that is bizarre but for some we were their Friday night escape. It was a ritual for some. A lot of people came to chat to Lorenzo, have a coffee while they waited for their pizza, just relax and be themselves. We learnt a lot about folks, their fears, their expectations, their problems, their travel plans, their sorrows, their joys. People opened up to us. It was more than just the pizza. I bump into a few here and there and what pleases me most is the way their eyes light up. It's motivating, it's real, it's humanity at its finest. It shows we held a place in their hearts. Well, maybe their bellies at least.

~ *Katia Macri-Roberts* ~

Here, there and everywhere

We love our staff. We really do. In case you haven't noticed, we have employed people from nearly every nationality, race, religion and sexual orientation. Some couldn't speak English, but that didn't matter, as long as the pizzas were fantastic. Hard work resulted in rewards, even a lab rat knows that. It's not rocket science. It all comes down to the staff. If you respect them, they will have respect for themselves and their work ethic. Most of our staff stayed with us for years and years and we appreciated their loyalty.

Even my own two children ended up with their first jobs working with their mother and grandfather. "Three generations working alongside each other" was our 2016 ad campaign. We even won the Foxtel "We Love Food" award on the Lifestyle Food channel for best family restaurant in Tasmania.

~ Secrets of Calabrisella ~

Nets, Chianti bottles and a blackboard no-one could read

Did you know the Spaghetti Marinara used to be served in foil shaped into a swan? A typical 70's New York style trend. We were one step away from fondue, I'm sure.

No matter how many people may whine on social media about places not moving with the times, we proved them all wrong. Lasting over 40 years with the one owner in a small town like Launceston. So many establishments came and went faster than you can say "balsamic glaze", which, incidentally, was the cliché band wagon we didn't jump on. Where else would you have a customer travel from interstate each year just to come in and order a plate of our carrots? Yes. No joke. This young lady remembers the carrots from her childhood and the taste must be a trigger for happy memories. A joy to behold, to be famous for a soft steamed carrot with our secret sweet sauce. No honey involved.

Back in the 80's, we had gargantuan nets draped from the ceiling. Chianti bottles lining the cornices. Lurid and ridiculous but it was authentic to say the very least. I guess it gave us character. Who remembers the cigarette bar? The milkshake corner? The school style blue bucket seats? The saloon half swing doors on the arches?

~ Katia Macri-Roberts ~

Every so often newspaper journos would do a write up for the weekend papers. They must have liked us, a lot. So many write-ups, at least 25 times according to the copious amounts of newspaper clippings adorning our walls. I'm sure the locals must have known our life-story years ago.

To quote one newspapers' finest :"It's casual and comfortable and every time you go, you seem to meet up with people you know". (Sounds like a bar on TV) "It's the kind of place where there's lots of table hopping and pulling tables together". He claimed we were his favourite restaurant in town. Not necessarily the best, but his favourite, and that to us, was what mattered. "I'm passionate about the pasta, crazy about the calamari, and voracious about the veal". From a food critic, it's always a pleasure to reminisce about how we tickled their fancies. Sounding a wee bit bashful, the accolades and the swirl of interest given to the community made us undeniably humbled.

Our Blackboards, the specials. People entered the room and made a bee-line for the board, in anticipation for what was different that week. Was it the fresh fish? Was it a different pasta? Tortellini? Gnocchi? Was it a new home-made torta? Hilariously people never realised most of dishes over time were the same but with a different name! Every Friday I had the arduous task of designing a new board. Some days I would re-hash a board from months prior, just fiddle-faddle with the ingredients a bit. Did anyone ever read the board carefully? I don't think so. Not many keen-eyed fans took note of the grandiose screed I was flaunting! But did you notice?

~ *Secrets of Calabrisella* ~

Vaya con Dias, my friend, Vaya con Dias

Over such a tremendous span of time there was bound to be some casualties. We remember our by-gone friends who will always be in our thoughts.

For one, the chilli connoisseur. I would put so much chilli in his pasta it would literally burn my eyes just placing it in the bowl. He loved it and always said I never put enough. Allergic to shellfish, but for 40 years had Spaghetti Marinara, go figure. He was a great pal to Lorenzo, and very sadly missed. Right back in the early times he and Lorenzo would wait with anticipation for the "new release" movies and would share the 'tapes'. Yes, tapes. No, not VHS, they came much later. These were Betamax. Even I remember the spaghetti westerns as a kid. We will never forget his cheeky, gruff, and to some, offensive attitude that everyone loved, nor will we forget that same old crumpled jacket.

At the time of writing, recently I was saddened to hear another long standing piece of our furniture (and I say that in the most respectful way) passed over to Eternal Rest. His claim to fame was that for 30 years he had over 1700 Marsalas. Our Veal Marsala, with extra sauce. Even his garlic pizza had to rolled thin as he walked through the door. We obliged of course. All washed down with a bottle of Lambrusca Rosso. Same order, each and every time, finished up with Kahlua with cream on top, a drink that is now my favourite. I hope you're not creating too much mischief up there, you cheeky bugger.

But we simply cannot go any further without a honourable mention to a special regular, may he Rest in Peace, who gave us the pleasure of serving him, his lovely wife, and their life-long theatre-going friends every week, right to the very end. Such a gentleman, and an inspiration for me, for it was he who instructed me to write these memoirs. I just wish he could have hung around a bit longer to embellish the fruits of my labour. We used to publish a different Italian proverb every week on our entrance board. His favourite was: "meglio un giorno da leone che cento da pecora". (Better to live one day as a lion than a hundred as a sheep.) By writing this book, I guess it's my "one day".

Of course there have been quite a few others, one minute they are splashing red wine all over our walls and the next they are unrecognizable with illness. Our advice? Live every day to the fullest. Eat the Tartufo.
Incidentally, the ever-loved chocolate icecream ball originated within Lorenzo's home province of Calabria. In a small town called Pizzo, not far from his local village. Hand made individually, the Tartufo is a succulent combination of chocolate and hazelnut gelati melded together encasing a decadent chocolate syrup inside. Akin to a hot molten lava cake, but a frozen delight in summer. treat to experience along the Calabrian coast.

~ *Secrets of Calabrisella* ~

Pass the Sunscreen per favore?

Now, a REAL Calabrisella devotee would know that we were never around in July. No Christmas in July, no "I'm cold, let's order pizza" in July, and definitely no Friday night football takeaways in July. Now, August was always a bumper month. A huge month as it was when we all re-appeared bronzed, mellow, and fat. Well, Lorenzo appeared in September but the rest of us plebs had to resume work to churn the moola again. Where were we hiding for a whole month or sometimes more? Despite in the early days, our signage said "renovations" but most people saw through that guise when we were sporting a suntan in winter. Our renovations usually consisted of moving some tables around and maybe a new picture hung, you know, major construction. Where were we?

We were in Italy. Tropea, Calabria to be exact. The "Coast of the Gods". A clifftop village winning the "Most beautiful town in Italy" award 2021. Its ancient ruins in the Old Town, to its famous red onions. Tropea is the backdrop for many celebrities trying to escape the paparazzi. Calabria is not the usual place for just anyone to holiday. Only the local Italian nationals spend their vacations here. It's rugged, off the beaten track, dangerous, dry, arid conditions, with a surfeit of hoodlums and racketeers. Quite frankly, I don't recommend anyone ever going there. Have I turned anyone off yet? It's so good to have a tranquil beach, with the bluest of blue water, the whitest of white sand, and the hottest sun with the most glorious sunsets. A place where tourists are oblivious of its beauty means everything is as it should be. Sometimes the best kept secrets are best kept secret.

~ *Katia Macri-Roberts* ~

For those that somehow managed to not notice the copious photos, paintings and artwork strategically placed around our walls, Tropea is a clifftop town on a beach from where all our seafood recipes originate. Well, mostly. Of course the Calamari Seviglia, Prawns Cordobesa and Mexicana all derive from their namesakes. Yes, we had a Latin feel. The vibrant Flamenco type music to the al frescos on the walls and the peasant charm of simplicity, it was all aimed at a classic experience to enhance the savoir-faire in all of us. For it was about closing your eyes, smelling the smells, hearing the music, gazing at the art, and immersing oneself in the culture of a faraway land.

This is your Captain speaking: Lets start from takeoff

From the time you board the aircraft, your mind, your body, your soul metamorphosizes to a realm of excitement that is almost impossible to illustrate. Lorenzo has been returning to Italy every year since the eighties. Myself regularly since the nineties. The twenty-four-hour flights injecting the purest of back pain, neck strain and insomnia will always somehow be a bane of my existence. Years ago, many of you will recollect the joy of the hot towels before the toilsome flight, the orange juice with the seemingly impossible to remove lid, and the excessively long wait for the 'new release' film on the one screen per cabin. Can you imagine it? No phones, no laptops, no internet. Just maybe a Walkman and a couple cassettes. We all couldn't wait to find out which movie was going to be broadcast on the flight. There was no way of knowing, a complete and utter surprise. Imagine that.

We always landed in Europe in the morning. Early morning, a glorious sunrise from the cabin windows just as we passed over Greece and Turkey we awakened from our uncomfortable, back-wrenching sleep. Racing to the bathroom before the hoards. The restrooms having just been freshly cleaned you could always smell the scent of lavender, a calming aroma for the feint hearted, apparently. Airlines like to use psychological warfare to calm the savage sleep deprived beasts with their fluid filled cankles.

As the plane makes it final approach, you hear the thud of the landing gear being set into place, the wing flaps extend, and the cabin crew scurry to prepare for landing. This is where you suddenly get excited, all the pain, angst and aggravation of the previous 24 to 30 hours seem to flutter away. It is now that English has disappeared and so too has organisation, order and harmony. In its place: chaos, erratic clutter, hustle and bustle, moped noise and profanities come to be the norm for the endurance of your vacation. Welcome to Italy. La Dolce Vita.

Imagine a decrepit old biddy scurrying through the alleyways of Rome barbarously muttering "Fanculo a te e al papa che ti ha portato qui!" Yes, she did suggest that I f*%k myself and the Pope that brought me to Rome. I recall it quite well, the European summer of 1999, the heat was overwhelming, the cobblestones hurting my feet, the smell of exhaust fumes and cigarettes with a slight whiff of coffee grinds wafting in every direction, and the rambunctious noise of the multitude of mopeds whizzing aimlessly in every direction. A cantankerous Lorenzo searching frantically for the Romanesque horse and carriage, which still, I might add, almost 25 years later, he hasn't ridden on. If you ask him, it is his ultimate aggravation. Stumbling into one of the plethora of alleyways in Rome, adjacent to St Peter's Square, the pearl of the Vatican, we inadvertently bombard our way into the tiny frail old woman lugging her groceries, her dog, and all her worldly possessions. It is here and now that we are told to f*&k ourselves. Perhaps if Lorenzo hadn't been mugged moments earlier, in his own native country, we might have been paying more attention. Let me divulge. Picture the scene, the family of six adults sight-seeing, it's uncomfortably hot. Tourists abound the Eternal city according to Tibullus in the 1st century BC, the "City of the Seven Hills", admiring the classic Baroque architecture. From the Colosseum to the Forum, the Pantheon to the infamous Fontana di Trevi, Lorenzo was our tour guide, even underground exploring the Catacombs. Then, close to the Termini, the main station in the crime ridden area, it happened. A group of filthy little girls, some would call gypsies, abruptly sidle up to Lorenzo begging for food clamping hold of dirty carboard. Their trick? The cardboard is held at waist height. The big puppy-dog eyes crying crocodile tears on their dirty faces languishing every part of your weary soul to give them any sort of morsal you can muster. Meanwhile, the minute mastermind behind rips into the back pockets of all your valuables, all whilst the "Romani" mother stands close by to reap the fruit of their deception. Alas, when Lorenzo felt a hand in his pant pocket, his quick reaction was to grab the girl and force her to drop the cash. It is now that the Roman cobblestones are littered with green plastic notes. Everywhere. Luckily for Lorenzo, the gypsy community did not know what these green notes were and scarpered extremely terrified. The equally filthy "mother' decided to spit on her darling children, pretending not to know a thing. Such a romantic city harbouring an equally diverse and conniving subset of humans. You see, these thieves, are known to 'earn' more money each day than you or I could ever dream of. Sigh, c'est la vie.

Lorenzo has a ritual now. Land at Fiumicino and get the hell outta there. Simple. It's the first plane, train or automobile and his compass points south. The Costa del Sol. The Coast of the Sun, his homeland, the place where his soul will always be. There has been many episodes of mishaps and disaster for dear Lorenzo. The seven hour car ride from Rome to Calabria is the bane of his existence. Was it the time he was hauling his family of eight in a very large minivan on the very narrow windy roads of the Amalfi coastline? Most likely. Getting a flat tyre half way up a mountain with the height of summers tourist traffic behind us led to some classic ribaldry. The family ejected to the side of the road for hours, in the hot Italian sun patiently awaiting a bewildered Lorenzo bearing gifts. Cannolis in fact. Yes, after a couple espressos, chitchat and pastries, he found a dude and a tyre. To this day we don't know what led him to sell his soul to the Devil that day. It was with wild jubilation and vivacity we finally reached our destination, safely, in one piece. Therefore, I'm sure this was the dawn of my vestibular vertigo.

~ *Secrets of Calabrisella* ~

Costa del Sol. The Road to Parghelia

Calabria is a place that is uninhibited, a place behind the times, some would say old fashioned, others archaic. The northerners shun the area as disadvantaged, pagan, and slow. But isn't that the dream? Isn't that what we all want, to take life easy? Unbridled landscapes of crisp air, warm sea and rural villages. The Calabrian coast, being somewhat iconic with breathtaking transparent aquamarine waters, white sand and spectacular cliffs boasts magnificent coves, inlets and majestic secluded beaches such as Michellino and Lido La Grazia. Monet, Manet and Renoir combined would have struggled to find a more picturesque canvas. Romantic yet sinister.

Parghelia is a one horse village on the coast, with spectacular clifftop views only a short distance to the magical seaside. "Paralija" as it was previously known in ancient Greek, is characterised by the giant rock aptly named 'La Pizzuta' or locally known as 'Il Palombaro', translated as "the deep sea diver". Many of these prominent protruding rocks have been named by the villagers over time. 'Scoglio di San Andrea', and 'Scoglio a Madonna' to name a couple. Lorenzo has fascinating memories of diving off these rocks and collecting an array of sea creatures. These waters are home to many sea urchins, white bait, squid, clams and of course, his favourite, limpets. Commonly

known as a sea snail, these conical abalone-looking "patellas" firmly attach themselves to the rocks. Limpet teeth, all 1,920 of them have considerable tensile strength. Needing superhuman force and a chisel or sharp flat rock will ultimately precure the culinary prize. These limpets are locally sourced for use in seafood pasta dishes as a relatively budget friendly meal for the local poor villagers. Lorenzo and his brothers enjoyed foraging around these rocks for items to bring back home to their mother to cook.

In 1905, a major earthquake destroyed the village except the local church that still stands today. This building is named the "The Church of Santa Maria di PortoSalvo". It boasts famous Neapolitan paintings such as the Annunciation, Sacra Famiglia (Holy Family) and the Madonna de Sette Delori (Our Lady of Seven Sorrows). The Madonna di

PortoSalvo is connected to the folklore of the seaside village that she will protect the inhabitants for their safety at sea. Each year, in August, the entire village parade through the streets behind an emblazoned portrait, a monolith painting of the Madonna to show their respects, their beliefs, and their wholehearted enthusiasms for their local heroine. A tradition celebrated by young and old, a truly captivating scene of a community banded together by faith. Lorenzo lived for this day of reckoning. He never returned to Australia until this day had been commemorated. Oh, and he always relished in jubilation over his saints day, August 10. The Patron saint of chefs, Saint Lorenzo. He always got

a cake from his mum. A day more special than his birthday. (If that could be possible) His family home in Parghelia will always be cherished and remembered by generations to come. I have brought my own children back here many times, and they have everlasting memories of side-walks lined with sun-drying tomatoes, fish markets, and Moroccan refugees selling their wares. A humble, peasant village in the middle of no-where, with donkeys and fresh mountain waterspouts has come to be an inaugural part of my provenance. This tiny village is only 500 metres from Tropea, the "Pearl of the Tyrrhenian" (recent winning town of the 'Borgo dei Borghi' the most beautiful village in Italy) is predominately renowned for its fishing and glorious sun kissed beaches on the Costa del Dai (Coast of the Gods). So, let's talk about Tropea, as every map, every tourist attraction and every gangster mob character will refer to this historic, uniquely preserved, Byzantine township.

This photogenic township with its panoramic views of the Tyrrhenian Sea offers anarray of architectural and historic delights. Boasting a 12th century Norman Cathedral, featuring a 4th century painting of the patron saint 'Madonna di Romania' who is archived to have saved the township from natural disasters. Byzantium, Roman and predominately Greek influences highlight the importance of art, culture and nobility of the 18th century. Unique, glistening sunsets propel your eyes toward the scenic views of Stromboli, the always fuming volcanic island in the near distance. The breath-taking hue of the brightest tangerine skyline would have to be one of the most photographed features of this glorious part of the world. The strategically placed viewing points of this clifftop town offer a full vista of the contours and rugged coastlines showcasing the turquoise warm waters abound. "Mozzafiato!!" is a phrase you will hear often. 'Breathtaking!!'.

The most abundant, somewhat iconic attraction is the glorious Santa Maria dell 'Isola—a 6th century Benedictine Monastery. This basilica-like structure juts out from the township like a mini peninsular, the clear blue waters surround it and the public can now climb the sandstone steps to visit the very place of worship for the monks of the Middle Ages. Unfortunately, during the earthquakes of 1783 and 1905, there is little of the original workmanship left, but the existing structure is notorious as the "Pearl of the Tyrrhenian".

The "Centro Storico" or the Old Town as it's lovingly known feature a medley of narrow cobble-stoned alleys, a sentiment of hidden surprises along the mishmash of collectable stores, hand-made ceramics and antiquities. Vast piazzas appear out of nowhere creating an illusion of pomp and opulence of the splendour from yesteryear. It is here one uncovers the most exquisite pastry shops, seafood restaurants and pizzas the south has to offer. A hidden gem, and a very well hidden one at that. It is here where you will be offered the homemade Limoncello after the meal as the 'Great Digestivo'. A drink of surprising medicinal qualities to say the very least. A citrus delicacy made with the sweetest lemons, sometimes a blood orange or even a loquat (nespolino). The alcohol volume is through the roof, akin to rocket fuel. Stored in the freezer, this delightfully cold, syrupy (yet not icy) nectar is a welcoming treat upon a sweltering summer evening.

Another is Amaro, a blend of digestive herbs and spices with a high alcohol volume. Amaro Del Capo is locally made and a signature of the Calabrian coast. Featuring bittersweet flavours of liquorice, elder berries, orange, aniseed, juniper berries, and chamomile, it is served chilled just like the Limoncello, a delightful after-dinner drink. Ideally sipping one whilst on the edge of the clifftop, gazing the sunset over the Tyrrhenian Sea on a hot August night. Who could forget the Aperol Spritz? The southern extravaganza as the Northerners love their Bellinis. But not everything revolves around alcohol, sometimes the best thirst quencher is a plain Latte di Mandorle. A very cold, very light almond cloudy cordial that looks like milk, served on ice and is a taste sensation!

So refreshing.

~ *Secrets of Calabrisella* ~

~ *Katia Macri-Roberts* ~

~ *Secrets of Calabrisella* ~

~ *Katia Macri-Roberts* ~

Until we meet again:

I said it before, and I'll say it again. Our customers were our family. Spanning four decades can bring a lot of memories for a huge part of the population. We remember you growing up. We remember when you got married. We remember when your children were born. We remember your birthdays, anniversaries and graduations. We remember the sad times when your parents and grandparents passed. We remember your first husbands and wives and celebrate your next stage in life. We have been labelled an iconic institution in Launceston and remain one of the longest standing businesses owned and operated by the same owner. For this we are proud and glad we could be a part of so many lives. We hope we have left a legacy for you, and your future generations.

Katia and Lorenzo

~ *Secrets of Calabrisella* ~

Recipes:

Here we have the part where I don't even want to call it the recipe section. Because they aren't real recipes. They are feelings. It's all about how it smells, how it feels, how it tastes. No Italian Nonna is going to hand out her family recipes willy-nilly. It's unheard of. An Italian grandmother will pass her secrets down to her daughter and her grand-daughter, and most definitely NOT to a stranger! However, some traditions can be replicated closely enough using the right amount of passion, enthusiasm and desire.

More often than not the meals are made with a handful of this, a shake of that, and a splash of something else that doesn't have a name, but is known in dialect. We second generations follow in awe, we just nod and try to keep up. The most important techniques are to feel, to see, to taste. It is my conjecture that the most intricate, long-winded, multi process "recipe" does not guarantee a perfect outcome. One must be immersed in the process, happy with the end result before completion, and most importantly, ready to experiment. It's all about those creative juices, and not falling into the trap of trying too hard. "A nervous hand will bear a failed cake". Most importantly understand that there is meaning to the phrase
 "Made with love".
       Que sera, sera. What will be, will be.

For us, it wasn't about grams, times, or measures. We just knew. It came from years and years of experience. I can't tell you how many mushrooms to cut up for Veal Marsala. I can't tell you how much cream to add to the Bora-Bora. This is what makes it real. You are making these in your home, for your family and your friends. Make it how you like. I'm just giving you some hints, some tricks, some secrets. Over the years dozens of people have tried to contact me begging for help with their Italian cooking. My advice is to close your eyes, bring your mind to Italy, inhale those aromas and anything is possible. You need to feel, smell and listen to the pan in front of you. Get in touch with all your senses and immerse yourself into the Italian culture. This is how each meal was made at Calabrisella. The following dishes are just a guide, it's up to you to provide those magic ingredients called love and patience to really succeed in any venture no matter what it is.

Now, addiamo a mangiare!! Let's go and eat!!

~ *Secrets of Calabrisella* ~

Stracciatella

Chicken Stock (Powdered)

One egg

Flat-leaf parsley

Pre-cooked filled pasta (tortellini or mini ravioli)

Salt/pepper

Parmesan Cheese

Who doesn't like chicken soup in winter? Or when feeling a general malaise? Well, we adapted the traditional consommé with tortellini and together with the long-established egg-drop soup we re-invented our take on the time-honoured stracciatella. Voila! Your thick, lustrous chicken, egg and cheese soup.

So, so easy.

If it's just for yourself or your special companion a small saucepan will suffice. (Add more water, eggs, pasta to suit added guests) Three-quarter fill the saucepan with hot water, add 5-6 Tortellini per person, and bring to boil. Once bubbling ferociously add the stock, as much or a little as you like. Boil for a few minutes. Whip (Or as Lorenzo used to always say "shake an egg") the egg, parmesan, salt, pepper and parsley together. Sometimes adding a dash of cream to the egg mix is a nice touch. Just before you are ready to serve slowly swirl the egg mix into the bubbling water, keep stirring for about 30 seconds or so. Serve hot with parmesan and parsley to garnish.

Enjoy with a loaf of Ciabatta on a cold winters night!

~ *Katia Macri-Roberts* ~

Spaghetti Amantea

Long Pasta (150g per person)
Sliced spring onions or chives
Sliced button or Swiss Brown mushrooms
Semi-dried Tomatoes
Thickened cream
Flat-leaf parsley
Garlic
Cracked Black pepper
Pecorino Cheese
Dry white wine (chardonnay)

One of our most popular dishes was the Amantea. A rich, creamy pasta with sun dried tomatoes, mushrooms and garlic.

Originally, we combined our homemade pesto into the collection of ingredients but we adapted the menu to exclude the pesto due to many people in the nineties suddenly having a morbid fear of nuts. Despite at the time pesto being one of the all-time ingredients du jour, (a bit like sriracha is these days) the nut allergy came up trumps, then of course gluten free, vegan and dairy-free emerged and became a now standard part of menus everywhere. However, we did adapt all our recipes to anyone that asked to the best of our ability. As 95% of our menu was NOT pre-made, we could do that. You order it, we made it, from scratch. People liked that. Didn't bother me in the kitchen, so why shouldn't we do it for the customer? Over the years I had some hilarious requests. Seriously? Wait, what? It was the highlight of my night to get some ridiculous order and then get the "Compliments to the chef" gaffe. I never knew really if it was tongue in cheek or not. Carbonara with olives and avocado was one. My Nonna would seriously be rolling about in her grave for sure.

We once had a waitress who ordered this dish by calling it A Man For Tea. It was the only way she could remember it. Geographically speaking Amantea is a delightful Calabrese town on the coast not far away from our own village. It is a township eclectic of castles and churches established by the Norman/Byzantium empires and most commonly affiliated with Joseph Bonaparte, brother of Napoleon, during a siege in the 19th century. This, the township, is what we named the dish after. NOT the highly toxic, poisonous amanita mushroom, by the way. To make this tasty dish, the secret is to simmer the sauce, continually adding wine if it gets too gluggy. Remember that.

If you don't have much wine on hand, adding the starch filled pasta water will suffice in creaming the dish. So, with any cream pasta dish, start cooking the pasta first. (The red/tomato sauces become more sweet and robust the longer they are cooked so make tomato sauces first) In another large pan, apply a generous knob of butter/margarine with some chopped flat leaf parsley and a handful of sliced spring onions. Low heat is always good. You have more control, and time not to get flustered. Add some garlic, crushed (in a jar) is good, or you can squish your own cloves of fresh garlic. Add a hand full of sliced mushrooms, Swiss browns having the best flavour. Moving the mushrooms around in the butter and letting them soak up the aroma of the garlic for a bit really gives the best outcome. Now, add a few semi-dried tomatoes, and some of the oil they came in. Not sun-dried, they are too hard and chewy and have a distinct dry texture. By now, heat can now be exhilarated just enough to hear a sizzling sound, it is at this point a good large splash of a dry white (chardonnay or sauv blanc) makes an appearance into the pan. Using the handle of the pan, swirl the ingredients around and around. The heat will be burning the alcohol off, but still infusing the ingredients with the flavours of the wine, the fruity full bodied acidic components will add a more robust palate. Now, once you can visibly see the liquid subsiding (this is a reduction) it is time to lower the heat again to a light simmer. Here we add cooking cream, or thickened cream. Swirl/stir again, and I find it best to add some parmesan now to thicken the sauce. A good quality one, aged and freshly grated if possible. Season with some cracked pepper and sea salt.

Grana Padano cheese is wonderful, so too is pecorino. Add some more chives and fresh flat parsley. By now your spaghetti would be al dente. I recommend carefully lifting your pasta out of the pot and placing it straight into your sauce. This way the fun-loving starch is still attached and will make its way to combing with the sauce to thicken and "cream" the dish. Add some salt, yes seasoning is a must. Stir and stir and stir and stir. I cannot emphasize this enough. The marriage of the pasta and sauce must be a happy one. A match made in Heaven, not one from Dante and his epitome of the fiery gates. So, if it's too thick, what do we do? Yes, more vino, or more starchy pasta water. That's why we don't drain the pasta away or you'll lose that magical water. Just add a bit, stir, add a bit more, stir. Till YOU think it's right for you. A nice adaptation is adding a little bit of tomato sugo, a Napoli sauce to the cream before the pasta is added. Just enough to give it a warm hue. And for all those leafy-green lovers, sometimes a good handful of fresh spinach is not only incredibly healthy but aesthetically pleasing. And, for those who wish to get all fancy, a swirl of expensive truffle oil on top will really get the juices flowing. Alternatively, a spoonful of mascarpone swirled into the pasta just before serving with add to the creamy sensation that your guests are craving.

~ Secrets of Calabrisella ~

𝓕𝓮𝓽𝓽𝓾𝓬𝓬𝓲𝓷𝓮 𝓜𝓸𝓷𝓽𝓮𝓫𝓮𝓵𝓵𝓸

Diced Pumpkin with Rosemary and Sea Salt

Red Capsicums

Fresh Spinach

Garlic

Spring Onions Sliced

Dry white wine

Thickened Cream

Good Quality Tomato sugo

Mozzarella/Parmesan

Long Pasta (150g per person)

Ahhhhh the Montebello. A newer edition to the menu, well, circa 2002. To us Italians everything is still new, even when it's pushing 20 years old it's still new with the plastic covering on, like the couch in Nonna's 'good room'. Translating to a 'beautiful mountain', it is the colourful mountain of fresh pasta before you. A hearty blend of roasted capsicum and baked pumpkin tossed with fresh spinach and creamy tomato gives it a splendid array of reds oranges, and green. A very popular dish for the vegetarians, and health conscious. For our vegan amigos, just omit the cheese and cream and voila.

In advance you will need to roast small pieces of pumpkin with some sea salt, cracked pepper and rosemary, drizzled with some virgin olive oil. A fabulous trick is to fold the vegetables with your hands, (yes, it's icky, but excellent outcome, trust me) making sure all the pumpkin is generously massaged in oil. Capsicums, you will need to bake them. Please use the red ones. For it is the red that have a more robust sweet flavour more appropriate for roasting. These will turn black. Don't freak out. Just gently peel back the black charred skin (which is bitter anyway) and you are good to go.

Okeydokey, starting with the staple ingredients, olive oil with a blob of butter in a pan, some fresh garlic, and some spring onions finely chopped. Sauté away gently. Add your pumpkin, and sliced capsicum pieces. Swirl them about in the pan, getting all that garlic to smother them. Now add a handful of fresh spinach. The leaves will sweat and shrink so don't be shy about how much you use, they will disappear quicker than a bad toupee in a hurricane.

Now, they all should be having a party in that pan, you should be wafting the delightful aroma of the Mediterranean. Now a little white wine, some tomato puree, or sugo. You can use your own chopped tomatoes fresh from the garden or a good quality passata sauce in a jar. (Our red sauce, Napoli, was made by simmering for hours and hours at a time. For these quick and easy dishes, a simple basil and garlic store bought sauce will suffice if time is of the essence.) Now add a generous swirl of cream. Let that simmer away gently while you cook your fresh pasta. Fettuccine is recommended, alternatively pappardelle or linguine.

Remember to add some of that starch water to the sauce to thicken and blend all the components together. Once the pasta has been added to the pan, a light sprinkle of sea salt, cracked pepper, and some grated parmesan and a handful of mozzarella cheese and Bob's your uncle. Easy peasy..Twirl and mix, and twirl and mix. It's like learning a dance. Repetition is the key to everything. Now a dash of cream and some flat leaf parsley and voila.
A mesa of colours ready to dazzle your dinner table.

Buon Appetito!

~ *Secrets of Calabrisella* ~

Rigatoni Fontana

Fresh chopped chillis
Garlic, diced onions, fresh basil
Flat-leaf Parsley
Pitted black olives
Spicy Hot Salami
Swiss Brown Mushrooms
Dry White wine
Good Quality Tomato sugo
Short Pasta (150g per person) Ideally Penne or Rigatoni
Parmesan or Pecorino

Fontana. A very agreeable, spicy dish with a robust, hearty amount of ingredients. Literally translated as a fountain. Initially thought to be the "fountain of youth", t'was the chilli bearing its tremendous height on the Scoville scale being the intrepid instigator of such archaic beliefs. Fresh chilli, home-grown and incredibly hot is best suited for this dish. Paring with piquant and zesty cured meats such as salami, makes for a celebrated and somewhat ambrosial collaboration of aromas and textures. For it is these flavours that Calabria is celebrated for in the culinary world, fiery hot chillies and pork salami (N'duja) . The combination of the two have earnt world-wide recognition for this N'duja, a thick spread made from red hot chillis and pork mince. A tiny near-by town (Spilinga) is famous for its creamy spreadable "salami". However, this delectable tongue-twinging delight is an optional ingredient and not for the faint-hearted. Let's get started.

Using a good quality virgin olive oil, line a large frypan generously. On a moderately low heat (best for keeping control of what you're doing.) add some chopped red or white onion, crushed garlic, and some chopped fresh chillies. Saute gently, you don't want your garlic to burn. It's a fine line between lightly sweating the onions and garlic to burn it and the pungent smell diffusing into the sauce unwittingly. Low heat, the key to success, and a blob of butter holds the secret to not burning the garlic.

Now it's time to add some sliced mushrooms. Be rustic. Slice them on the thick side, as mushrooms tend to disintegrate and lose their structure easily. Add some black olives, pitted of course, we don't want any extra visits to the dentist, do we?

Remember to toss, to swirl, to jostle the frypan with gusto. We want an even distribution of flavours, we don't want all the chilli and garlic holding onto dear life in the corner. We now must add the star of the show, your salami. Mild or piquant, it is the chefs prerogative to forge their creation. Saute saute saute, constantly moving the ingredients. It is now you have full control. You are not side-tracked by gathering fundamental elements. You have it all in your hands now so turn the heat up. Yes, you need to embark on the road to flambe now. You would be hearing the sweet sound of sizzle. It is now you splash some chardonnay. It will smoke a bit, don't panic this is normal. Jostle and swirl this heavenly liquid you have before you. Once the steam has risen, the alcohol is reducing. Gently add your tomato sauce, preferably a good quality Italian sugo.

Now you simmer. Turn the heat down. Let those flavours immerse themselves within. Allowing it to simmer for as long as possible provides for the greatest of results, ensuring an adequate amount of seasoning is given. Sea salt is wonderful for this. Whilst it is fricasseeing away, now would be a good time to add some flat-leaf parsley and basil to give that sensation of colour.

Time to cook your pasta. Penne or Rigatoni are the most ideal shapes, or any short pasta available. Calabrese folk generally use homemade "fileja" , a shape originating from our home region of Vibo Valencia. The shape is accommodating to a hearty, meat containing sauce like this one. Once your pasta is al dente, gently add to your sauce. Remembering the starchy water is highly recommended to add to your sauce, a little here and there to combine and thicken your creation.

Using your large spoon or tongs, swirl your pasta generously for this ensures the sauce is evenly distributed. Another trick is to undercook the pasta and consequently leave in the sauce for longer to enrich and enhance those flavours. Finally, a good grating of pecorino cheese and fresh basil and enjoy!

~ Secrets of Calabrisella ~

Spaghetti Bora Bora

Black Tiger Prawns

Mussels, cleaned

Fresh scallops (Tasmanian if available)

Baby clams

Smoked Tasmanian (Atlantic) Salmon

Calamari (squid) strips, scored

Garlic / Black Pepper

Shallots / Flat leaf parsley

Long pasta

Cream

Dry white wine

Bora Bora, French Polynesia, where it all began. The orange juice stand to be precise. A gallant Lorenzo picked up a bashful Sherryll off the floor, literally. For she had tripped and fallen. From this moment on, was the inauguration of the lovestruck besotted duo. For this union in the tropics became the birth of Spaghetti Bora Bora, an emblematic token of their unexpected tryst. Let us now discover how to recreate this spectacular fare.

One of the most popular dishes in our repertoire, this creamy yet delicate array of fine seafood is complimented with a hint of garlic and black pepper. Many people tend to surmise that making pasta is easy. Yes. Yes, it is easy, but making good, flavourful pasta is a little trickier. It's the art of knowing when to add the wine, when to flambe the garlic, when to add the pasta. Slight imperfections of timing results in soggy, waterlogged tasteless slop and I cannot stress this enough.

Preparing the seafood is quite easy. De-shelling the prawns and scoring the squid would be most important. Cutting the squid into large, thick rings, then making one cut into a long strip. Using a sharp knife, mark the soft blubbery side (as opposed to the shiny side) with diagonal lines, repeat the opposite direction to make crosses. This enables all the garlic goodness to penetrate and enhance the flavours throughout.

We start by using a knob of butter and a little garlic. One or two crushed cloves will suffice. Low heat ensures the garlic does not burn. For if it does, you will never get that lingering stench out of the meal. Watching intensely, you can always add a splash of white wine at that toasting point. This will sizzle in the pan, which is fine, just ensure complete evaporation so as not to boil the seafood we are about to embrace. Add some shallots or finely diced brown onions and flat leaf parsley. Gently sweat the new additions and add the seafood. A generous sprinkle of sea salt and black pepper. Raise the heat a little, not too much, you still need to have control. Using a wooded spoon or tongs, turn the ingredients over and over to disperse the garlic and onions evenly. Seafood does not take long to cook, literally a couple of minutes. Over cooking results in chewy, bland calamari and we do not desire that. It is now another splash of wine, and a dash of cream creates a light sauce. Lower the heat and add our long pasta. Spaghetti or linguine work best to savour the flavours of the sea. Season again and add more parsley.

Although you will never see an Italian place cheese on a seafood dish, sometimes a good pecorino will act as a thickener to make a creamier sauce. Adding the starchy pasta water is another alternative, and widely used. As an alternative, instead of the cream, replace with fresh chopped tomatoes, basil and olive oil. Voila, you have Marinara !

~ *Secrets of Calabrisella* ~

Mussels Arrabiata

Cleaned Fresh Blue Lipped Mussels (or Green lipped)
Crushed garlic, chopped onions and celery
Finely chopped red chillies
Liquid chicken stock
Shallots and flat leaf parsley for flavour
Tin of good quality chopped tomatoes
Dry white wine
Salt and Black Pepper for seasoning
Fresh Basil

Now this truly has to be the Magnum Opus of our specials board. Simple, no fuss, no stress yet seemingly intricate masterpiece provides so much awe at a dinner party. Ridiculous really, as Europeans delightfully order this dish at the local beach as Australians would a pie with sauce. With the capability of envisaging your own heat, one can concoct an inferno Dante himself would find himself to be bashfully corrected. Alternatively, a sparing amount of chilli, or even none at all for those that would prefer a stroll through the dewy meadows of surety.

A winters haven, this "Zuppa di Cozze" (Mussel soup) is a must just to warm the cockles. Not really a soup per se, more of a meal. Loads of mussels, small amount of broth. Starting with some olive oil in a deep pan, sweat the onions, celery, chilli and garlic on a medium heat until they begin to slightly turn light brown in colour. Hearing the sizzle, splash some of the wine. Right about now you will hear a louder sizzle and some steam will arise. This is perfect. Move the ingredients constantly to ensure even heat coverage and to ensure evaporation of the alcohol volume. Turn the heat down to low and add the tomatoes. Fresh tomatoes (Roma or home-grown cherry) are perfect in summer but if not available a good quality Italian tin is just fine. Season with black pepper and sea-salt. Slowly add the stock as the sauce will be starting to thicken up. This is a broth so the texture needs to be thin and delicate. Slightly raise the heat and then add the mussels. If fresh, they will be whole. They will slowly open up as they heat. Some places do sell half shells which is neither here nor there as you will be providing the flavour with your chilli and garlic quantities. Sprinkle your shallots, basil and parsley for a colour pop. After about five minutes of simmering, stirring and blending those spices and flavours together the dish is ready to impress. Serve with ciabatta bread, enjoy!

~ Katia Macri-Roberts ~

~ Secrets of Calabrisella ~

Gamberi Giannini

De-Veined Black Tiger Prawns

Crushed garlic

Diced onion

Pine nuts

Sweet chilli sauce

Spring onions/flat leaf parsley

Dry white wine

Salt and black pepper

Plain flour (Omit for gluten free)

Cooking Cream

Gamberi Giannini. The name says it all. Named after my two children, this dish had some interesting pronunciations. A blend of their two names, it was most humorous to me to hear people say they love this dish, they have it wherever they go. I once heard a man gloat that he has it all over Europe. This surprised me as I had made it up. It was then that I was intrigued. I researched and to my fascination I found guitar makers, bankers, coffee machines and football players but no prawns, no food in fact apart from a remote restaurant in Malta. Albeit a truly successful dish without knowing it, the notoriety was overwhelming.

Using a medium sized frypan, place a knob of butter, parsley, onions and garlic into the pan on medium heat. Listening to the sizzle, swirl the melting butter to the edges to ensure complete coverage. Sweat the onions until golden. Toss in the pine nuts. Stir all ingredients with a wooden spoon, ensuring the nuts do not burn. Once a toasted look appears, lower the heat. Meanwhile, lightly flour the prawns. Make sure they are dry to start with. Nothing worse than claggy, soggy wet flour which will ruin the texture of the sauce. Place the prawns into the pan and gently flip the ingredients around. Make them dance. Don't be shy, get those prawns moving. Splash some wine, sprinkle some salt and pepper, and pour a little (or a lot) of sweet chilli sauce. Right about now, the aroma of garlic, chilli and the sensation of flambeed wine should be filling your kitchen. Your delicate senses should be in overdrive and a heightened array of olfactory emotions will prevail. Prawns do not take long to cook, I always butterfly slice them so I know when they curl inside out and turn pink, they are ready to rumble. Add a dash of cream, swirl and serve immediately with buttered greens like broccolini, or asparagus. Some rosemary infused baked sweet potato blends in perfectly with this awesome, simple dish.

~ *Secrets of Calabrisella* ~

Chicken Cacciatora

Chicken breasts, filleted.

Black olives, pitted, capers

Button mushrooms

Garlic, parsley, basil, diced onions

Red wine, good quality crushed tomatoes

Salt/pepper

Olive oil/butter

Literally translating to "hunter", this dish is prominent in the rustic bushlands of country Italy. A winter dish sometimes featuring rabbit instead of chicken. A popular item on our menu, the Cacciatora is easily made and pairs wonderfully with a ciabatta loaf and a good Chianti.

In a large fry pan, on medium heat, brown the floured chicken breasts in olive oil and a small amount of butter. Season with salt and pepper and sprinkle some parsley to flavour. Set aside to rest. Turning the heat down, gently sweat the olives, onions, garlic and mushrooms. Add some more butter if needed. Swirl the pan to get those juices flowing, letting the ingredients dance a little in the pan. Once browned a little, add the chicken back into the pan. Turn the heat up a bit and add the chopped tomatoes, capers and basil. When you hear the sizzle, this is when you pour the rich nectar of the red wine over the chicken. Swirl everything. This will enhance the red wine jus that is now starting to form. Turn the heat down and simmer gently for about 20 minutes ensuring the chicken is soft and tender but most importantly cooked through.

At any time you feel it needs more sauce or it is drying up, just gently and slowly add more wine or a bit of warm water or both. Not too much as the desired result should be a thick rich stew type dish. Serve with a mash and buttered greens.

Bellisima!

~ *Katia Macri-Roberts* ~

Melanzane alla Parmigiana

(*Eggplant Parmesan*)

2 large Eggplants
6 boiled eggs
Mozzarella and freshly grated Parmesan
Salt
Paper towel
Virgin olive oil
Diced Onion, crushed garlic, fresh basil, flat leaf parsley
Tin of good quality crushed tomatoes
Jar of good quality tomato sugo

This Calabrese classic is a staple found on most menus within the antipasto section. More specifically the part of the menu most locals focus strongly upon, the "antipasto della casa" or 'home-made appetisers. Some of you will glance and fixate on the word "parmigiana" and immediately think chicken, with chips and a pint of beer. Sadly, you will be mistaken but hopefully after further divulging in the fascination of Calabrese fare you may be politely swayed into the vegetarian cousin I bring before you.

There are many speculations about the origin of the name, however most lead to the fact Parmigiano-Reggiano cheese is the topical ingredient. Despite this cheese influenced dish deriving from the Northern province of Parma, melanzane alla parmigiana is known to have origins dating back solely to the Southern regions, namely Calabria, Sicily and Campania.

Some would call this a vegetarian lasagna, utilising the eggplant as the pasta sheets. A simple, yet effective layering technique enables full flavour enhancement in every portion. Easily prepared ahead, this dish will win over the non-carnivores in your dinner party, and apart from placing in the oven, you can let the fiddle-faddle minutia occupy your day before so as to let you enjoy the festivities.

To begin, slice the eggplant into circles approximately 1cm thick. Not too thin they break, and not too thick you need a chainsaw to eat the meal with. Place onto a large area, preferably a cutting board. Sprinkle salt (and don't be shy) and leave for about an hour. This brings out the copious amounts of water in the fruit that could potentially drown the dish later. Incidentally, every Calabrese nonna will also advise that this process takes away the severe bitterness that the eggplant tends to have. While this sweating process is doing its

~ Secrets of Calabrisella ~

thing, now is a great time to prepare the Napoli sauce, or sugo.
In a large saucepan place the diced onion, garlic and some virgin olive oil. On moderate heat, lightly brown the onion, without scorching the garlic. Add the crushed tomatoes, basil and parsley. Stir, and add the jar of sugo. Season lightly (remember the eggplant is having a salt sauna behind you) and lower the heat. Simmer away til needed. Boil the eggs for 6-7 minutes for a glorious hard boiled egg. Peel and slice.

Back to the eggplants, using paper towels, gently blot dry, both sides of the 'rounds'. The star of the show should now be ready to bake. Alternatively you can shallow fry but I find that process time consuming, less healthy and more expensive as it uses a vast quantity of oil. Bake on a large flat foil-lined tray in a moderate oven until golden brown. While baking, the sugo should be simmering away nicely.

Now comes the assembly. Quick, easy and by now you should be getting excited. Using a baking dish, place some of the red sauce on the base. Layer your eggplants and cover with cheese. Add a layer of sauce, layer the egg slices and repeat the process, ending up with tomato sugo and cheese on the top. Sprinkle more basil and cover with foil. When required, bake for about one hour on a medium setting. A good idea is to let stand for about 10-15 minutes (like a lasagna) for easy sectioning and plating. Enjoy with crumbed lamb cutlets, or maybe some rosemary infused baked chicken pieces? A star-studded dish flying solo or coupled with something more substantial. The culinary world is your oyster!

~ *Katia Macri-Roberts* ~

Cotoletta Bolognese

Fresh Veal fillets, tenderised and sinew removed.
Bread crumbs
Egg, flat leaf parsley, garlic, parmesan cheese, salt, pepper, flour
Mozzarella
Home-made Bolognese Sauce
Virgin Olive oil

Crumbed veal topped with our famous Bolognese sauce and mozzarella baked in our pizza oven. One of our most popular dishes indeed. Simple yet effective. Yes these days anyone can buy a beef schnitzel at the supermarket but it will never have the flavours of the Mediterranean in the crumb, the soft melt-in-your-mouth fillet of veal, or the classic secrets of our Bolognese seductively adorning the cutlet.

Using proper first grade veal is number one priority for tenderness. Using beef, even if you can get it sliced thin will not engage those gustatory sensations that are imperious for classic cuisine of this kind. Be that as it may, true veal is sometimes hard to come by but if you can land your hands on a fillet or two consider yourself among the opulent.

Historically speaking, this dish is not generally found among the region of southern Italy. In fact, not a lot of meat dishes are locally sourced. Finding a butcher in the mountain villages of Calabria is like asking someone the directions to the end of a rainbow. Impossible to find.

Southern provinces such as Campania, Calabria and Sicily are generally known for their fish and pork specialties. There are an abundance of pig farms where the best chilli laced sausages are locally produced. You can drive for miles and miles through the rugged coastlines of Calabria, up into the deep mountains and never see a cow. Or a sheep for that matter.

Back to the Cololetta, a staple of the Northern region. Generally known as "Milanese" the crumbed veal cutlet normally is void of any sauce. Just a squeeze of a juicy lemon and voila. Plain and somewhat boring so we decided to add some pizazz to it, as we do.

~ Secrets of Calabrisella ~

In a small bowl, crack the egg, add a generous amount of parmesan, parsley, crushed garlic, salt and pepper. Whisk. Once you have your tenderized veal fillets (you can easily place on a board with cling wrap and use a rolling pin if you don't have a meat tenderizer) lightly flour them beforedrenching them in the egg wash. Then it's just a hop skip and a jump into the breadcrumbs. A good idea is to wear food handling gloves, saves getting gunk in your rings. Once the fillet is in the crumbs, I like to punch the veal. Yes you read that correctly. I find that it helps the crumbs to stick evenly while adding more tenderising making it softer. It also helps vent any frustrations. Quite a good therapy, clears the mind. A messy but fun job.

Once all cutlets are crumbed, lightly pan fry in virgin olive oil on a medium heat. Alternatively, on a hot grill if you have one. When golden brown, they are ready to top with a generous amount of pre-prepared Bolognese sauce and mozzarella cheese.

Then into a hot oven to melt the cheese to a golden colour. Sprinkle with more parsley and enjoy with a nice Mesclun salad.

~ *Katia Macri-Roberts* ~

Limoncello Tiramisu

Savoiardi biscuits (Ladyfingers)
500g Marscapone cheese
One cup Fine Sugar
Limoncello Liquor (Homemade or store bought)
Thickened cream
Lemon zest / juice
Limoncello Liquor

Ahhhhh, what meal would be complete without the taste of lemon? Lemon Sorbet is a splendiferous finale and palate refresher, however only welcoming in the summer months. This show-stopper can arouse all year long with it's tangy sweet yet light and fluffy Southern Italian take on the traditional Tiramisu.

Originating in the Veneto Region of Northern Italy, the classic Tiramisu (Pick-me-up) consists of caffeine infused biscuits. Some later recipes have added alcohol such as Marsala or Amaretto to make it even more alluring. This is a lemon creation, however if you prefer the traditional coffee flavours you can easily replace anything 'lemon' with hot strong coffee and Marsala liquor.

To re-create this lemon 'piece de resistance', place sugar and mascarpone into an electric beater bowl and beat on a moderate speed until the sugar is nicely ground into the creamy cheese. Squeeze some lemon juice to smooth the mixture and to add a citrus twang. Slowly pour in the thickened cream and turn up the speed to a fast beat. Whip until thick. Splash in some Limoncello to spice up the taste. Optional: grate some lemon zest for added flavour. In a saucepan, pour some lemon juice, Limoncello, a little warm water and add some sugar. Stir over low heat until sugar is dissolved. This will be the syrup for the biscuits. Using a nice glass oblong baking dish, drizzle some of the syrup onto the

~ Secrets of Calabrisella ~

base. Not too much, just enough to soak into the bottom of the biscuits. Methodically dip the ladyfingers into the warm syrup to cover each biscuit and then place length ways into the dish. Once the base is filled with soaked biscuits, pour half the creamy whip over and smooth down with a spatula. Repeat another layer of biscuits and whip. Drizzle some syrup over the biscuits before the whip layer if you feel the liquid has not penetrated thoroughly enough. Grate some more lemon zest on top to decorate. It is important to rest dessert in the refrigerator overnight to fully appreciate the lemon liquor soaking into the sweet biscuits for maximum flavour.

Buon Appetito!!

~ *Katia Macri-Roberts* ~

Torta Cassata Siciliana

(Easy version)

1kg Fresh Ricotta

Dark chocolate chips

Almond Essence

Icing sugar & water (or lemon juice) for Royal Icing

Candied orange/pineapple/cherries

2 blocks of Easy roll marzipan

Green food colouring or Pistachio syrup

Orange flavoured liquor (Grand Marnier or Cointreau)

Pre packaged sponge cake or make your own vanilla sponge.

Typically known as a Sicilian delight, this crème de la crème dessert is often found in up-market Pasticceria's around Calabria. Uniquely described as a very difficult creation, most people avoid making it at home and prefer to pay the big bucks to a pastry-chef for a joyous occasion or celebration. That being said, I have made this several times, for it is Lorenzo's favourite cake in the world. And yes, each time I've made it, it still hasn't lived up to the splendour that Calabria brings to his taste buds. Don't get me wrong, he devours every bit of it, and does not share, but as he will always point out, the Australian ricotta does not come anywhere near the quality of what is available in Italy. The ricotta is the star of this show, so please try to find the best you can and don't skimp as it will truly show in the end result.

I have chosen to print the easy "cheats" way to create this dish. Using pre-packaged cake, pre-packaged marzipan and pre-candied fruit will literally save you hours. Traditionally this unique confection takes several, if not more, hours to prepare. I've managed to beat it down to less than one hour. You can thank me later.

So, everyone knows "Cassata". Immediately ice-cream springs to mind, with crushed nuts, glace fruit and an almond flavour. Yes, habitually originating from Sicily, it's a matter of which came first, chicken or the egg. According to history, it was the torta that was born into Italian culture from several origins, namely Spain and Arabic introduction. The word Cassata is derived from the Arabic "quas'at" meaning 'wide circular pan with sloping sides'. The cake, highlighting chocolate, sponge and candied fruit depict a Baroque influence. Literal translations turn up as 'Pan di Spagna' (Bread from Spain).

~ Secrets of Calabrisella ~

One main characteristic of this Saracen sweet is that it was commonly consumed solely at Easter, to celebrate the end of the Lenten period. Now a glamourous treat for any special occasion.

Take a deep breath, clear your workspace, and chill. It's a little fiddly but the reward is splendiferous! Firstly, you will need a round bowl, like a pie dish with flared edges. Approximately 30cm in diameter.

In a large mixing bowl, place the ricotta, chocolate chips, candied orange peel and some icing sugar (not too much, but if you don't put any the dessert may be a bit tart) and combine with a wooden spoon. Add some almond essence and I like to put a bit of the liquor in too. Oh, by the way, this dessert is VERY adults only. Quite a bit of high-volume alcohol is used. (Well, in mine it is....) Mix well, it must be thick, not runny at all as this is the middle of the cake. Cover and set aside in the fridge to amalgamate the flavour intensity.

Now, spread a heap of flour out on your work bench and onto your rolling pin. You will need to roll out the marzipan into sheets about the thickness of a pastry sheet you would use to make a pie. One block will remain white. The other block, once you have softened it a bit, you need to add some green colouring and/or pistachio essence. Once it turns a lime colour, it is ready to roll flat.

Using a sharp knife, cut the marzipan pastry into long rectangles about the width of the height of your cake pan. (Probably 2 inches wide, if the pan is 2 inches tall). Here you will then cut the rectangle into smaller trapezoid pieces. Do this for both the white and the green marzipan. Sprinkle the pan well with icing sugar (or use cling wrap). Place the trapezoids using alternating colours around the side edge of the pan. One upright, the next upside down, then upright and so on.

Once you have a ring of multi-coloured marzipan around the edge of the pan, now add your sponge. You will need to cut it accordingly to fit the base of the pan first. If it is a round sponge, slice lengthways to produce two cake discs. Place the first into the pan to fit snug. Drizzle with your liquor. Not too much to drench it as it still needs to be firm to hold its form. Next, scoop your ricotta mix into the pan almost filling it to the top. Smooth it over.

Finally, before adding your second cake disc on top, drizzle some liquor on it and place it face down onto the ricotta mix. Place cling wrap over the top and refrigerate for 24 hours to let the alcohol soak through the cake.

After its sojourn in the fridge, this is where it may be tricky. For now is the time to flip. Yes, it's really an upside-down cake. The bottom layer is really the top.

Place a large plate on top of the pan and turn upside down. It should easily slip out of the pan right-side up. Now, prepare the Royal icing by mixing icing sugar, a small amount of warm water or lemon/orange juice to a consistent homogenous paste and pour gently over the entirety of the cake, sides and all.

Let harden and decorate with candied oranges, pineapples, figs, pears and cherries. Sometimes a small piping bag of icing can be used to "draw" intricate squiggles around the sides for an added regal look.

If you managed this far and haven't drunk the bottle of Cointreau, kudos to you. Revel in your masterpiece and savour that eclectic blend of Arabic goodness since the 10th century!

~ *Secrets of Calabrisella* ~

To conclude our repertoire of culinary delights, we leave you with a quote from Lorenzo's late mother, the Matriarch of the Macri-Mamone family, a toast she said before every momentous meal:

*"Questo vino e bello e fino
E viene da una lunga via
Io brindo gli faccio
a questa bella compagnia!"*

*(This wine is beautiful and
it comes from a long way
I toast to us
To this beautiful companionship)*

Gioconda Mamone 1922-2018

Acknowledgements:

Historical facts - Tropea, Parghelia, Amantea and other parts of Calabria:

- *Calabria Museo Archeologico guida fotografica e storica* by Rosella Vantaggi 1996
- *Proverbi Calabresi* by Francesco Spezzano 2010
- Editorial content – *The Examiner* Newspaper, Launceston 1980 through to 2020, (*Fairstar* clipping circa 1972) and *Italianicious* magazine Jan 2015.
- Photos by Katia, except those credited to A.Vallone.

About the Author

Katia is a talented "Jill of all trades" successfully obtaining a Masters in Hairdressing and Commercial Cookery, both of which she has excelled in for over 30 years. Working two careers and raising a family simultaneously Katia understands the requirement for some quick and easy homestyle Italian recipes.

Being a travel connoisseur, Katia, with her husband Ian, have circumnavigated the globe many times over, family in tow, exploring the rugged hidden gems of Calabria as a specialty destination. Combining her flair for cooking and creative hair artistry she is highly regarded amongst her colleagues and clientele in both professions.

In her spare time, she enjoys walking her sled dog Siberian Husky and meticulously researching her family tree, currently tracing family back to early 1300's.

Figure 2 Photo credit:A.Vallone

www.ingramcontent.com/pod-product-compliance
Lightning Source LLC
Chambersburg PA
CBHW040315240426
43663CB00025B/2977